PREFACE

The fifty items in *Carols for Choirs 3* have been chosen to serve the needs of a wide range of occasions: carol services, Christmas concerts, end-of-term school events, and carol singing in the open air. Twenty-nine items are suitable for unaccompanied singing; they range from simple four-part settings to more ambitious extended arrangements. Many of the others have accompaniments for orchestra, in most cases calling for only modest resources. Details are given in the Index of Orchestrations, and parts are available on hire. Some items have accompaniments for small instrumental ensembles and thus may be especially useful in schools. In every case, however, piano or organ accompaniment is quite adequate.

As with *Carols for Choirs 1 and 2*, the backbone of the present collection is the great wealth of traditional carols that have come down to us. A number of these have been newly arranged by the Editors, some in simple unaccompanied versions that provide an alternative to more extended or elaborate ones previously available. Two medieval carols are included, and five examples of Baroque Christmas music, by Monteverdi, Praetorius (2), Charpentier, and J. S. Bach.

A Christmas anthem by Herbert Howells and a carol by William Walton were specially commissioned for this volume; other twentieth-century composers represented include Richard Rodney Bennett, Benjamin Britten, Gustav Holst, and William Mathias. Three carols, *Birthday Carol*, *Star Carol*, and *I saw three ships*, specially written or arranged by the Editors for the annual Bach Choir Family Carol Concerts at the Royal Albert Hall have refrains which may be sung by a chorus of children who can be taught the melody at the time of performance. Extended arrangements of an Advent and an Epiphany hymn are included, together with four-part versions of *O come, all ye faithful* and *Hark! the herald angels sing* – both indispensable to any Christmas collection. *This joyful Eastertide*, which appears as an appendix, is possibly the only Easter carol to have gained wide popularity and will, it is hoped, be a useful inclusion.

There is a further appendix, a list of Christmas readings suitable for use in programmes of readings and music as an alternative to the Advent and Christmas Services of Lessons and Carols (see *Carols for Choirs 2 and 1* respectively).

The repertoire performed by choirs is continually broadening, and *Carols for Choirs 3* seeks to reflect an increasing diversity of styles and periods, while remaining within the capacity of an average group of amateur performers.

© OXFORD UNIVERSITY PRESS 1978

INDEX OF TITLES AND FIRST LINES

Where first lines differ from titles the former are shown in italics.

Carols suitable for unaccompanied singing are marked thus*.
Carols with orchestral material available on hire are marked thus†.
(*Details of orchestrations are given in the separate index on p.199.*)

4

commissioned by the Cardiff Polyphonic Choir in association with the Welsh Arts Council

1. A BABE IS BORN

Words: 15th century, anon.

WILLIAM MATHIAS
(Opus 55)

†ORGAN

†or Piano duet, with 2nd player taking the pedal part only.

Printed in Great Britain

him   we sing both night and day.

Ve - ni Cre - a - tor Spi - ri - tus,

Ve - ni Cre - a - tor Spi - ri - tus,

Ve - ni Cre - a - tor Spi - ri - tus.

3. There came three kings out ___ of the East, ___ To wor-ship the King that ___ is so free, With gold and myrrh and frank - in - cense, ___ A so - lis ___ or - -

A so - lis or - tus car - di -

A so - lis or - tus car - di - ne, ___ car - di -

so - lis or - tus car - di - ne,   car - di - ne,   car - di - ne,   car - di - ne.

-ne,   car - di - ne,   car - di - ne,   car - di - ne,   car - di - ne.

-ne,   car - di - ne,   car - di - ne,   car - di - ne,   car - di - ne.

- - tus   car - di - ne,   car - di - ne,   car - di - ne,   car - di - ne.

4. The an - gels came down___ with one   cry,

A fair   song___ that night

Man.

sung___ they In wor - ship___ of that child:___

Glo-ri - a ti - bi Do - mi - ne,

Ped.

Glo-ri - a ti - bi Do - mi-ne,   Glo-ri - a ti - bi Do - mi-ne,

Glo-ri-a ti-bi Do - mi-ne,   Glo - ri - a,   glo - ri - a,

glo - ri - a,   glo - ri - a.

Man.

5. A

babe is born all _ of a may,_____ To

bring sal-va-tion _ un-to us. To

him we sing both night and day.

2. A BABE IS BORN IN BETHLEHEM

Words tr. by
G. R. WOODWARD

German traditional carol
Harmony by J. H. SCHEIN (1586—1630)

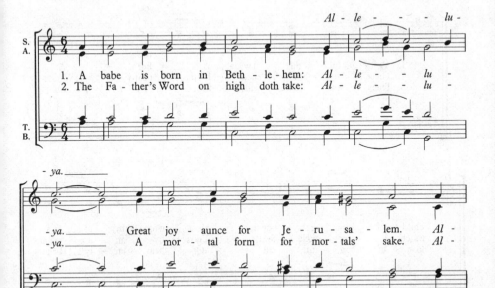

1. A babe is born in Beth - le - hem: *Al - le - - lu -*
2. The Fa - ther's Word on high doth take: *Al - le - - lu -*

- ya. Great joy - aunce for Je - ru - sa - lem. *Al -*
- ya. A mor - tal form for mor - tals' sake. *Al -*

- le - lu - ya, al - le - - lu - ya.
- le - lu - ya, al - le - - lu - ya.

3. Through Gabriel his greeting mild
The Virgin hath conceiv'd a child.

4. He took our flesh, to man akin,
In all things like us, save in sin.

5. Both ox and ass, though beasts they be,
Yet in that child their master see.

6. Now, Yule-tide come, sing high, sing low.
Benedicamus Domino.

7. To thee, good Lord, be glory paid,
Thou babe of Mary, mother-maid.

8. To Holy Trinity give praise,
With *Deo gracias* always.

Original pitch a tone lower.

3. A CHILD THIS DAY IS BORN

English traditional carol
arranged by DAVID WILLCOCKS

4. They praised the Lord our God,
   And our celestial King:
   All glory be in paradise
   This heav'nly host do sing.

5. All glory be to God,
   That sitteth still on high,
   With praises and with triumph great,
   And joyful melody.

Optional Descant

No - well,   No - well,   No -

REFRAIN

No - well, No - well, No - well,   No -

- well sing all we may,   Be - cause the King of

- well sing all   we   may,   Be - cause the King of

all____ kings Was born up - on__ this   day.

all____ kings Was born__ up - on this__ day.

for Michael Nicholas and the choir of St. Matthew's Church, Northampton

4. SUSANNI

Words: 14th century

RICHARD RODNEY BENNETT

A lit – tle child there is y – born, Ei – a, ei – a,

su – san – ni, su – san – ni, su – san – ni. And he sprang out of

Al – le – lu – ya, al – le – lu – ya.

Jes-se's thorn, To save all us that

were for – lorn. Now Je – sus is the child – es name,

No. 5 of *Five Carols*, reprinted by permission of Universal Edition

5. THREE EXTRACTS FROM
CHRISTMAS ORATORIO

1. Chorale: Ah! dearest Jesu

Words tr. by
REVD J. TROUTBECK

J. S. BACH

Ah! dear - est Je - su, _ ho - ly child,

Make thee _ a _ bed, soft, _ un - de - filed,

2. Pastoral Symphony
Score and parts are available on hire.

3. Chorale: With all thy hosts

With all thy— hosts,— O— Lord,— we— sing,

And— thanks and— praise— to— thee— we—

6. ANGELUS AD VIRGINEM

(Gabriel to Mary came)

English translation by
W. A. C. PICKARD-CAMBRIDGE★

14th century
arranged by DAVID WILLCOCKS

T.B. 1. An - ge-lus ad vir - gi-nem Sub - in - trans in— con - cla - ve,
  1. Ga - bri-el to Ma - ry came, And en - tered at— her dwell - ing,
S.A. 2. 'Quo - mo-do con - ci - pe-rem Quae vi - rum non— co - gno - vi?
  2. 'How could I a mo - ther be That am to man— a stran - ger?

Vir - gi-nis for - mi - di-nem De - mul - cens, in - quit, 'A - ve!
With his sal - u - ta - tion glad Her maid - en fears— dis - pel - ling,
Qua - li - ter in - frin - ge-rem Quod fir - ma men - te vo - vi?'
How should I my strong re-solve, My sol - emn vows— en - dan - ger?'

★Slightly adapted

© Oxford University Press 1978

D.S. Verse 2

7. FLEMISH CAROL

Words translated by
R. C. TREVELYAN

Flemish traditional melody
arranged by
JOHN RUTTER

1. A lit - tle child on the earth has been born, A

lit - tle child on the earth has been born; He came to the

Also available separately (X213)
Words from *The Oxford Book of Carols* by permission

all,   He   came to   the   earth for the   sake   of   us   all.

TENORS and BASSES **C**

2. He   came   to   earth but no   home did he   find,   He

came   to   earth but no   home did he   find,   He   came__   to   earth and its

cross did he   bear,   He   came__   to   earth and its   cross did he   bear.

ALL VOICES   **E**

f crisply

3. He came to earth for the sake of us

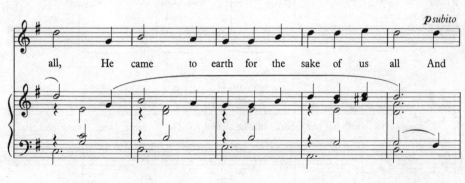

all, He came to earth for the sake of us all And

p subito

wish - es us all a hap - py New Year, And wish - es us

for Simon Lindley and the Choir of St. Albans School

Traditional words

8. SUNNY BANK

Music by
PETER HURFORD

As I sat on a sun - ny bank, On Christ - mas Day in the morn - ing, I spied three ships come sail - ing by, On Christ - mas Day in the morn - ing. On Christ - mas Day, on Christ - mas Day, On Christ - mas Day in the morn -

Also available separately (X 250)

© Oxford University Press 1975

*This descant may be whistled by a few, good, musical, accurate whistlers, if desired.

joy that our Sa - viour   he was born,   On Christ - mas Day in the morn -

On   Christ - mas Day,   on   Christ - mas Day,

- ing.   On   Christ - mas Day,   on   Christ - mas Day,   On

allarg.

Christ-mas Day in the morn - ing, On Christ-mas Day in the morn - ing.

allarg.

l.h.

9. BETHLEHEM, OF NOBLEST CITIES

(Earth has many a noble city)

Words by
PRUDENTIUS (b. 348)

Adapted from a melody in
Psalmodia Sacra, Gotha, 1715
Last verse arranged by DAVID WILLCOCKS

Words from *The English Hymnal*:

1 Bethlehem, of noblest cities
  None can once with thee compare;
Thou alone the Lord from heaven
  Didst for us incarnate bear.

2 Fairer than the sun at morning
  Was the star that told his birth;
To the lands their God announcing,
  Hid beneath a form of earth.

3 By its lambent beauty guided
  See the eastern kings appear;
See them bend, their gifts to offer,
  Gifts of incense, gold and myrrh.

4 Solemn things of mystic meaning:
  Incense doth the God disclose,
Gold a royal child proclaimeth,
  Myrrh a future tomb foreshows.

5 Holy Jesu, in thy brightness
  To the Gentile world displayed,
With the Father and the Spirit
  Endless praise to thee be paid.   Amen.

Translation by E. CASWALL (1814—1878)

Words from *Hymns Ancient and Modern*:

1 Earth has many a noble city;
  Bethlem, thou dost all excel:
Out of thee the Lord from heaven
  Came to rule his Israel.

2 Fairer than the sun at morning
  Was the star that told his birth,
To the world its God announcing
  Seen in fleshly form on earth.

3 Eastern sages at his cradle
  Make oblations rich and rare;
See them give, in deep devotion,
  Gold and frankincense and myrrh.

4 Sacred gifts of mystic meaning:
  Incense doth their God disclose,
Gold the King of Kings proclaimeth,
  Myrrh his sepulchre foreshows.

5 Jesu, whom the Gentiles worshipped
  At thy glad Epiphany,
Unto thee with God the Father
  And the Spirit glory be.   Amen.

Translation by E. CASWALL (1814—1878)
and the compilers of *A. & M.*

*Congregation and part of choir sing the melody.

10. CHILD IN A MANGER

Words by
JOHN RUTTER

Celtic traditional carol
arranged by JOHN RUTTER

*Left-hand part may be played by any suitable instrument. If clarinet is used in v.1, bassoon could be used in v.2. (A fully scored version is also available on hire.)

© Oxford University Press 1978

Led by a star.

Ah

Of - fer your trea - sures: Gold, myrrh, and in - cense,

Ah

Pre-cious ob - la - tions   Brought from a - far.

p cresc. - - - - - -

f

4. Praise to the Christ - child;   Praise to his mo - ther; —

f

mf   *f*

11. CHRIST WAS BORN ON CHRISTMAS DAY

Words by
J. M. NEALE

Old German tune
arranged by DAVID WILLCOCKS

12. CHRISTE, REDEMPTOR OMNIUM

Christmas Office Hymn
(6th century)

CLAUDIO MONTEVERDI
(1567 – 1643)

from *Selva morale e spirituale* (1640)

Original note-values divided by eight. Barring, small notes, and the introduction, are editorial.

★may alternatively be sung by sopranos an octave higher

*may alternatively be sung by sopranos an octave higher

13. COME ALL YOU WORTHY GENTLEMEN

Words collected by
CECIL SHARP

Old English tune
arranged by DAVID WILLCOCKS

1. Come all you wor-thy gen - tle-men that may be stand-ing by,
2. Christ our bless-ed Sa - viour now in the man-ger lay. He's
3. God bless the ru - ler of this house, and long on may he reign,

Christ our bless-ed Sa - viour was born on Christ-mas Day.
ly - ing in the man - ger while ox - en feed on hay.
Ma - ny hap - py Christ-mas-ses he live to see a - gain!

The bless-ed Vir-gin Ma - ry un - to the Lord did pray. O we
The bless-ed Vir-gin Ma - ry un - to the Lord did pray. O we
God bless our ge - ne - ra - tion, who live both far and near, And we

wish you the com - fort and ti - dings of joy!
wish you the com - fort and ti - dings of joy!
wish them a hap - py, a hap - py New Year!

14. COME, ROCK THE CRADLE FOR HIM

Words by
G. R. WOODWARD

*Psalteriolum
Harmonicum*, 1642

1. Come, rock the cra - dle for him, Come, in the crib a - dore him, Dull care, I pray you, bu - ry, And in the Lord make mer - - ry. *Sweet lit - tle Jesu, sweet lit - tle Jesu.*

2. Come, rock his cradle lowly,
The throne of God all-holy:
Come worship and adore him,
And kneel we down before him.
    Sweet little Jesu, sweet little Jesu.

3. Nor come with empty coffer,
But thanks and blessing offer;
Let old and young be merry,
And blithe as bird on berry.
    Sweet little Jesu, sweet little Jesu.

4. And sing, for music-number
Will lull the babe to slumber:
Your strain be sweet and airy,
Like that of blessèd Mary.
    Sweet little Jesu, sweet little Jesu.

5. Do nothing to annoy him,
But everything to joy him;
For sin, by night or morrow,
Would cause him pain and sorrow.
    Sweet little Jesu, sweet little Jesu.

6. So at your hour of dying,
This babe, in cradle lying,
(For he is King supernal)
Shall grant you rest eternal.
    Sweet little Jesu, sweet little Jesu.

Words reprinted from *The Cowley Carol Book* by permission of A. R. Mowbray & Co. Ltd.

15. DECK THE HALL

Welsh traditional carol
arranged by DAVID WILLCOCKS

1. Deck the hall with boughs of hol - ly,
2. See the flow - ing bowl be - fore us,
3. Fast a - way the old year pass - es,

Fa la la la la, fa la la la,

'Tis the sea - son to be jol - ly,
Strike the harp and join the cho - rus,
Hail the new, ye lads and las - ses,

Fa la la la la, fa la la la.

Fill the mead cup, drain the bar - rel,
Fol - low me in mer - ry mea - sure,
Laugh - ing, quaff - ing all to - ge - ther,

Fa la la la, fa la la la,

Fill the mead cup, drain the bar - rel,
Fol - low me in mer - ry mea - sure,
Laugh - ing, quaff - ing all to - ge - ther,

Fa, fa la la la la,

Troll the an - cient Christ - mas ca - rol,
While I sing of beau - ty's trea - sure,
Heed - less of the wind and wea - ther,

Fa la la la, fa

Fa la la, fa la la la la.
fa
fa la

for Simon Lindley and the Choir of St. Albans School

16. DONKEY CAROL

Words and music by
JOHN RUTTER

Also available separately (X254) and in an arrangement for S.A. (T111)

3. Don – key rest – ing all in a manger stall,_____

Hum_____

Hum_____

Hum_____

With the ox – en wor-ship the Lord of all._____

Hush, he lies a – sleep on his bed of hay While Ma – ry

lul - la - lay.'

mp

sings so sweet – ly 'Lul - la, lul – la,___ lul - la, lul – la –

mp

17. HARK! THE HERALD ANGELS SING

Words by C. WESLEY,
T. WHITEFIELD, M. MADAN
and others

MENDELSSOHN,
adapted by W. H. CUMMINGS

For version with descant by David Willcocks, see *Carols for Choirs 1*.

Deity pronounced Dee-ity

18. WEXFORD CAROL

Irish traditional carol
arranged by
JOHN RUTTER

Andante con moto

mp flowing and expressive

BARITONE
SOLO
(or full Basses)

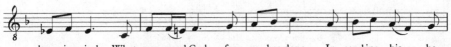

1. Good peo - ple_ all, this Christ-mas-time, Con - si - der well_ and

bear in mind What our good God for us has done, In send-ing his_ be -

-lov - ed Son. With Ma-ry ho - ly we should pray To_ God with love_ this

S.

pp legato

A.

Hum

T.

B.

pp legato

Christ-mas Day; In Beth-le - hem up - on that morn There was a bless-ed Mes-

Melody and words used by permission of The Very Rev. W. G. Canon Flood
This setting may be sung a semitone higher.

CHOIR I { Verse 2: SOPRANOS (and ALTOS)
         { Verse 3: TENORS (and BASSES)

mf dolce

-si - ah born.

2. The night be - fore   that
3. Near Beth - le - hem   did

p   *sempre legato*

CHOIR II   Aw___   2. Aw___   Aw___   Aw___   Aw___
            ___ 3. Ah___   Ah___   Ah___   Ah___

p *sempre legato* 2. Aw___   Aw___   Aw___
                    3. Ah   Ah___   Ah___

hap - py tide   The no - ble Vir - gin and her guide   Were
shep-herds keep Their flocks of lambs___ and feed-ing sheep;   To

long time seek - ing up and down   To find a lodg - ing
whom God's an - gels did ap - pear,   Which put the shep - herds

___   Aw_____   Aw___
___   Ah_____   Ah___

___   Aw_____
___   Ah_____

in the town. But mark how all____ things came to pass: From
in great fear. 'Pre - pare and go',____ the an - gels said, 'To_

Aw
Ah

ev - 'ry door__ re - pell'd, a - las! As long fore - told, their
Beth - le - hem,_ be not a - fraid; For there you'll find, this

refuge all Was but an hum - ble ox - en stall.
hap - py morn, A prince - ly babe, sweet Je - sus born.'

4. With

CHOIRS
I and II

for Simon Lindley and the Choir of St. Albans School

19. JESUS CHILD

Words and music by
JOHN RUTTER

Also available separately (X244) and in an arrangement for unison voices (U156)

S. {1. Je - sus child?
A. /2. flocks at night?

Have you heard the sto - ry of the Je - sus child? How___ he
Sit - ting on the hill - side with their flocks at night?_ Sud - den -

heard the sto - ry of the Je - sus child?
on the hill - side with their flocks at night?

S. {How he came from hea - ven and was born in a man - ger bed?
A. {Sud - den - ly the an - gel tells them: 'Hur - ry to Beth - le - hem;

- hea - ven and was born in a man - ger bed?
came from - an - gel tells them: 'Hur - ry to Beth - le - hem;
- ly the

How he came from hea - ven and was born in a man - ger, Ma - ry
Sud - den - ly the an - gel tells them: 'Hur - ry to Beth - le - hem;_

cresc.

Ma - ry was his vir - gin mo - ther pure and mild.___
Go and find the Je - sus child, the world's new light.'___

cresc.

was his vir - gin mo - ther pure and mild.___
Go and find the child, the world's new light.'_

cresc.

'Glo - ry   to   God   on   high'   the

praise his   mo – ther mild. _____   'Glo – ry   to   God'   the

an – gel   hosts   a – bove   are   sing – ing:

dim. _ _ _ _ _ _ _ _ _ _ _ _ _ _ _ _ _ _ 𝆏 non stacc.

an - gel _____ hosts   are   sing – ing: Lis – ten   to   the   sto – ry   of   the

dim. _ _ _ _ _ _ _ _ _ _ _ _ _ _ _ _ _ 𝆏 non stacc.

dim. _ _ _ _ _ _ _ _ _ _ _ _ _ 𝆏

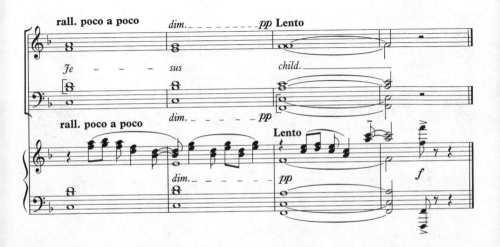

rall. poco a poco   dim. _ _ _ _ _ _ _ _ _ pp **Lento**

Je _ _ _ _ sus   child. _____

dim. _ _ _ _ _ _ pp

rall. poco a poco   dim. _ _ _ _ _ _ _ pp   **Lento**

dim. _ _ _ _ pp

𝆑

20. HE SMILES WITHIN HIS CRADLE
(The Cradle)

Words Austrian, 1649
Tr. ROBERT GRAVES

Austrian melody
arranged by DAVID WILLCOCKS

1. He smiles with-in his cra - dle, A babe with face so bright It beams most like a mir - ror A - gainst a

3. And who would rock the cra - dle Where-in this in - fant lies, Must rock with ea - sy mo - tion And watch with

to next page for Verse 4

blaze_ of light: This babe_ so burn - ing bright.____
hum - ble eyes,____ Like Ma - ry pure_ and wise.____

lul - la, lul - - - - la, lul - la - by.____
lul - la, lul - la,

- la, lul - la, lul - la - by.____

2. This babe_ we now de - clare_ to you Is Je - sus Christ_ our

poco cresc.

Lord;____ He brings_ both peace and heart - i - ness: Haste, haste with

poco cresc.

D.C. for Verse 3

one_ ac - cord____ To feast_ with Christ_ our Lord.____
To feast, to

To feast, to

21. HUSH! MY DEAR, LIE STILL AND SLUMBER

Words by
ISAAC WATTS

French melody
arranged by
DAVID WILLCOCKS

Recommended pronunciation of Lullaby = *Loo-la-by.*

2. Sleep, my babe; thy food and rai - ment, House and home, thy friends pro -
4. Soft and ea - sy is thy cra - dle; Coarse and hard thy Sa - viour
6. Lo, he slum-bers in his man - ger, Where the horn-ed ox - en

SOLO ALTO (or A.1 TUTTI)

- vide;   All with-out thy care and pay - ment, All thy wants are
lay   When his birth-place was a sta - ble And his soft - est
fed;   Peace, my dar - ling! here's no dan - ger; Here's no ox a -

well   sup - plied.
bed   was hay.
near   thy bed.   Lul - la, lul - la, lul - la,

lul - la - by.   Lul - la, lul - la, lul - la - by.
lul - la, lul - la, lul - la, lul - la, lul - la - by.
lul - la, lul - la - by.   Lul - la, lul - la, lul - la - by.

to next page for verses 3 and 5
for verse 7 turn to p.92

Back to previous page
for verses 4 and 6

*2nd Sop. and 2nd Ten. may be omitted.

22. IN THE BLEAK MID-WINTER

Words by
CHRISTINA ROSSETTI

In moderate time

SOPRANO
ALTO

1. In the bleak mid - winter   Fros-ty wind made moan,___
2. Our God, heav'n can-not hold him   Nor___ earth sus - tain;___
3. E - nough for him, whom che-ru-bim   Wor-ship night and day,___ A
4. An - gels and arch - an - gels   May have ga-thered there,___
5. What___ can I give___ him,   Poor___ as I am?___

TENOR
BASS

Earth stood hard as i - ron,   Wa - ter like a stone;
Heav'n and earth shall flee a - way   When he comes to reign:
breast - ful of milk,___ And a   man - ger - ful of hay;   E -
Che - ru - bim and se - ra-phim   Thronged___ the___ air: But
If I were a shep - herd   I would bring a lamb;

Snow had fal - len, snow on snow,   Snow___ on___ snow,   The
In the bleak mid - win - ter A   sta - ble - place suf - ficed   The
- nough for him, whom an - gels   Fall___ down be - fore,   The
on - ly his mo - ther   In her maid-en bliss   The
If I were a wise___ man   I would do my part;   Yet

In the bleak mid - win - ter,   Long___ a - go.
Lord___ God Al - might - y   Je - sus___ Christ.
ox and ass and ca - mel   Which___ a - dore.
Wor - shipped the Be - lov - ed   With___ a kiss.
what I can I give him —   Give___ my___ heart.

Reprinted by permission of Oxford University Press and G. & I. Holst Ltd.

for Sir David Willcocks and The Bach Choir

23. I SAW THREE SHIPS

English traditional carol
arranged by JOHN RUTTER

This arrangement is designed to allow the participation of children, who are taught the melody at the time of performance.

for The King's Singers

24. IL EST NÉ LE DIVIN ENFANT

(He is born the divine Christ-child)

English words by
DAVID WILLCOCKS

French traditional carol
arranged by DAVID WILLCOCKS

★divin pronounced di-veen

(After Refrain following Verse 4,
go to Coda p. 105)

D.S.

poco rit. *(a tempo)*

2. Ah, qu'il est beau, qu'il__ est char-mant, Qu'il est doux, ce di-vin en-fant!
4. O Jé - sus, roi__ tout puis-sant, Rég-nez sur nous__ en-tière-ment.
2. O what   beau-ty and charm are thine,   O what sweet-ness thou Child di - vine!__
4. Je-su,   King, whom we bow be-fore,   Rule our hearts now and ev - er - more.__

D.S. *(a tempo)*

mp

La la la la la.

D.S. *(a tempo)*

p

né,_____ né,___ né,_____ né!
born,_____ born,___ born,_____ born!

D.S. *(a tempo)*

p

né,_____ né!_____
born,_____ born!_____

CODA

pp *ppp*

S.
A.

est   né!
is   born!

pp *ppp*

T.
Bar.

est   né!
is   born!

f   *mf*   *p*   *pp*   *ppp*

B.1

Il est né, il est né, il est né, est né!
He is born, he is born, he is born, is born!

f   *mf*   *p*   *pp*   *ppp*

B.2

Il est né, il est né, il est né, est né!
He is born, he is born, he is born, is born!

25. ANGEL TIDINGS

Words by
JOHN RUTTER

Moravian traditional carol
arranged by
JOHN RUTTER

Arrangement from *Eight Christmas Carols* (Set 1) by John Rutter (OUP)

Christ our Lord.

Ah

F ALL VOICES
mp crisply

4. Sing then and be joy - ful on this Christ - mas night; Fol - low with the

8ve

wise _ men the star so bright; Lead you to his own glo - ry, Tell out the

cresc. _ _ _ mf legato

26. CRADLE SONG

Words by
JOHN RUTTER

Flemish traditional carol
arranged by
JOHN RUTTER

Melody reprinted by permission of Schott Frères (Brussels).

This setting may be sung a semitone lower, if preferred.

lul - - la - by,___ lul - la,___ lul - la, lul - la - by.

lul - la - by, lul - la, lul - la, lul - la - by.

lit - tle one sleep; An - gels round you watch will keep.

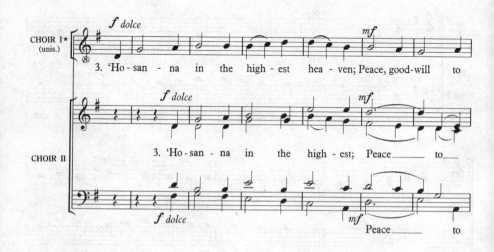

CHOIR I★
(unis.)

3. 'Ho - san - na in the high - est hea - ven; Peace, good-will to

CHOIR II

3. 'Ho - san - na in the high - est; Peace___ to

Peace___ to

men on earth.' Se - ra - phim on high__ in cho - rus Greet the

earth.' Se - ra - phim on high, se - ra - phim on high Greet the

men__ on earth.'___ Se - ra - phim in cho - rus Greet_ the

★If preferred, Choir I part may be sung by a solo voice, in which case Choir II should sing 'Ah' or hum.

Sa-viour's joy-ful birth.   Ma-ry's voice, in des-cant blend-ing,

Sa-viour's joy-ful birth._____   Ma-ry's voice, in des-cant

Joins_ the heav'n-ly song un-end-ing: Lul-la-by, O

blend-ing, Joins_ the song un-end-ing: Lul-la-by,_____

lit-tle one sleep;   An-gels round you watch will keep.

lul-la,_ lul-la-by;_____   An-gels watch_ will keep.

27. IN DULCI JUBILO

English translation by
R. L. PEARSALL

Old German carol
arranged by
JOHN RUTTER

Arrangement from *Eight Christmas Carols* (Set 1) by John Rutter (OUP)

*A few sopranos and tenors, or solo voice

(SEMI-CHORUS REJOIN OTHERS)

-ae! Tra - he me post te! tra - he me post te!

Ah

Ah Ah

Ah Ah

Ah

8ve-

3. O

pp

B

p legato

Ah

Pa - tris car - i - tas, O Na - ti le - ni - tas!

B

mp

28. ALL IN THE MORNING

English traditional carol
arranged by R. VAUGHAN WILLIAMS

1. It was on Christ-mas Day,
2. It was on New Year's Day,

And all in the morn - ing, Our Saviour was born,
They cir - cum - cised our Sa - viour And our heav'n - ly King:

And was not this a joy - ful thing? And sweet Je - sus they called him by name.

3. It was on the Twelfth Day,
   And all in the morning,
   The wise men were led
   To our heav'nly King:

   And was not this, etc.

4. It was on Twentieth Day,
   And all in the morning,
   The wise men returned
   From our heav'nly King:

   And was not this, etc.

5. It was on Candlemas Day,
   And all in the morning,
   They visited the Temple
   With our heav'nly King:

   And was not this, etc.

29. KING JESUS HATH A GARDEN

Words translated by
G. R. WOODWARD

Dutch traditional carol
arranged by JOHN RUTTER

1. King Je-sus hath a gar-den full of di - vers flow'rs, Where

I go cull-ing po-sies gay, all times___ and hours. *There*

Words reprinted by permission of A. R. Mowbray & Co. Ltd.

SOPRANOS *mp dolce*

2. The   li - ly, white in   blos-som there is   chas - ti -
li   -   ly,   in

ALTOS   *mp dolce*

dim. - - - *p*

- ty: _____ The   vi - o - let with sweet per - fume, hu - mi - li -

- ty. _____ S. *p stacc.*

A.
There naught   is   heard   but   pa - ra - dise   bird,   Harp,

T.

B.
p stacc.

p

legato

And the ten - der sooth - ing flute; With cym - bal,

legato   flute;   *mf* With cym - bal,

trump and tym - bal, And the ten - der sooth - ing___ flute.___

trump,   *legato*   *p*

legato

E *mf*

Ah ___

f unis.

4. Yet, 'mid the brave, the bra - vest prize of all may

S.

A.

Ah ___

Ah ___

T. and B.

Pno.

claim   The   Star of Beth - lem — Je - sus — Bless - ed   be___ his

5. Ah! Je - su Lord, my heal and weal, my bliss com - plete, Make thou my heart thy gar - den-plot, fair, trim and neat. That I may hear this

30. LO! HE COMES WITH CLOUDS DESCENDING

Words by C. WESLEY
and J. CENNICK

18th-century English melody
Last verse arranged by DAVID WILLCOCKS

1. Lo! he comes with clouds descending, Once for fa-voured
Thou-sand thou-sand saints at-tend-ing Swell the tri-umph

sin-ners slain; Al-le-lu-ia! Al-le-lu-ia!
of his train:

(to next page for Verse 4)

Al-le-lu-ia! God ap-pears, on earth to reign.

2. Every eye shall now behold him
Robed in dreadful majesty;
Those who set at nought and sold him,
Pierced and nailed him to the tree,
Deeply wailing *(3 times)*
Shall the true Messiah see.

3. Those dear tokens of his passion.
Still his dazzling body bears,
Cause of endless exultation .
To his ransomed worshippers:
With what rapture *(3 times)*
Gaze we on those glorious scars!
(to next page for Verse 4)

Harmony for verses 1—3 from *The English Hymnal*

31. O COME, ALL YE FAITHFUL

(Adeste fideles)

Words by J. F. WADE
tr. F. OAKELEY, W. T. BROOKE
and others

Melody by
J. F. WADE (c. 1711–1786)

1. O come, all ye faith - ful, Joy - ful and tri - um - phant, O come ye, O come ye to Beth - le - hem; Come and be - hold him Born the King of An - gels: O come, let us a - dore him, O come, let us a - dore him, O come, let us a - dore him, Christ the Lord!

2. God of God, Light of Light, Lo! he ab - hors not the Vir - gin's womb; Ve - ry God, Be - got - ten, not cre - a - ted:

3. See how the shep - herds, Sum - moned to his cra - dle, Leav - ing their flocks, draw nigh with low - ly fear; We too will thi - ther Bend our joy - ful foot - steps:

4. Sing, choirs of an - gels, Sing in ex - ul - ta - tion, Sing, all ye cit - i - zens of heav'n a - bove; Glo - ry to God In the high - est:

Harmony from *The English Hymnal*
For extended version arranged by David Willcocks, see *Carols for Choirs 1.*

32. O LITTLE TOWN OF BETHLEHEM

(original version)

Words from St. Luke 2, vv. 11, 12
and by PHILLIPS BROOKS

WALFORD DAVIES

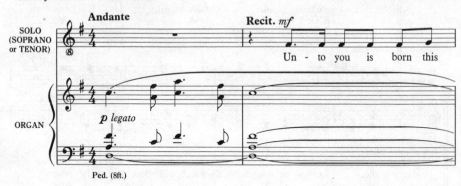

The original piano accompaniment adapted for organ by David Willcocks by permission.

140   Davies: O little town of Bethlehem

(a tempo)

dream-less sleep The_ si - lent stars go by. Yet_ in thy dark streets shin - eth The_ ev - er - last - ing light; The hopes and fears of all_ the_ years Are met___ in thee to - night.

2. How si - lent-ly, how si - lent-ly, The

Poco meno mosso

Ped. (16ft.) to Sw.

poco sostenuto

3. O   ho - ly Child of __ Beth - le - hem, Des - cend to us, we__ pray; Cast__

out our_ sin, and__ en - ter _ in, Be _ born in__ us to - day. We__ hear the Christ-mas_

an   - gels The _ great glad ti - dings tell: O _ come to us, a - bide with us, Our

Lord__ Em - man - - u - el.   (voices tacent)

Em - man - u - - el.

O LITTLE TOWN OF BETHLEHEM

(version for unaccompanied singing)

Words by
PHILLIPS BROOKS

WALFORD DAVIES

1. O lit-tle town of Beth-le-hem, How still we see thee lie!
2. For Christ is born of Ma-ry; And, ga-ther'd all a-bove,
3. How si-lent-ly, how si-lent-ly, The won-drous gift is giv'n!
4. O ho-ly Child of Beth-le-hem, Des-cend to us, we pray;

A-bove thy deep and dream-less sleep The si-lent stars go by.
While mor-tals sleep, the an-gels keep Their watch of wond-'ring love.
So God im-parts to hu-man hearts The bless-ings of his heav'n.
Cast out our sin, and en-ter in, Be born in us to-day.

Yet in thy dark streets shi-neth The ev-er-last-ing light;
O morn-ing stars, to-geth-er Pro-claim the ho-ly birth,
No ear may hear his com-ing; But in this world of sin,
We hear the Christ-mas an-gels The great glad ti-dings tell:

The hopes and fears of all the years Are met in thee to-night.
And prais-es sing to God the King, And peace to men on earth!
Where meek souls will re-ceive him, still The dear Christ en-ters in.
O come to us, a-bide with us, Our Lord Em-man-u-el.

33. OMNIS MUNDUS JOCUNDETUR

(Earth this glad day rejoices)

Medieval Christmas hymn
English words by JOHN RUTTER

MICHAEL PRAETORIUS
(from Musae Sioniae, 1607)

Original pitch a major third lower; note values quartered.

Chri-stus na-tus ex Ma-ri-a vir-gi-ne, vir-gi-ne, vir-gi-ne,
Chri-stus na-tus ex Ma-ri-a vir-gi-ne, vir-gi-ne, vir-gi-ne.

Vir-, vir-gi-ne; gau-de-te, gau-de-te,
To his bless — ed mo-ther mild let us pray, let us pray;

Gau-de-a-mus et lae-te-mur i-ta-que, i-ta-que, i-ta-que,
Al-le-lu-ia! Chri-stus na-tus ho-di-e, ho-di-e, ho-di-e;

- que.
- e.

i-ta-, i-ta-, i-ta-, i-ta-, i-ta-que, i - - ta-que.
Chri-stus na-tus, Chri-stus na-tus ho - di - e, ho - - di - e.
i-ta-, i-ta-, i-ta-, i-ta-, i-ta-que, i - ta - que.
Chri-stus na-tus, Chri-stus na-tus ho - di - e, ho - - di - e.

34. PSALLITE UNIGENITO

English words by
JOHN RUTTER

MICHAEL PRAETORIUS
(from *Musae Sioniae*, 1609)

Original pitch a tone lower. Verse 2 added editorially.

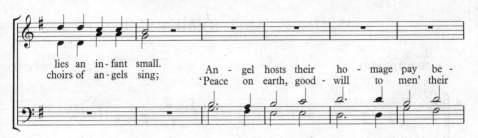

lies an in-fant small.
choirs of an-gels sing;

An - gel hosts their ho - mage pay be -
'Peace on earth, good-will to men' their

An - gel hosts their ho - mage
'Peace on earth, good - will to

-fore the Lord of all, low be - fore him fall.
voi - ces ech - o - ing, praise the new - born King.

pay be - fore the Lord of all.
men' their voi - ces ech - o - ing. Psal - li - te

Psal - li - te

Psal - li - te

Psal - li - te

after vv. 1 and 2:
D.S.

u - ni - ge - ni - to Chri - sto De - i Fi - li - o,
u - ni - ge - ni - to

35. ONCE, AS I REMEMBER

Words by
G. R. WOODWARD

Italian carol
arranged by
CHARLES WOOD

1. Once, as I re-mem-ber, At the time of Yule,
2. Near as man was a-ble, On my knee fell I,
3. Ox and ass a-round him, Court-ier-like, did stand:
4. E-v'ra-mong and o'er us An-gel-quire 'gan sing

Af-ter mid-De-cem-ber, When it blow-eth cool,
In the Beth-lem sta-ble Where the babe did lie,
Fair white li-nen bound him, Spun by Ma-ry's hand,
An-ti-phons in cho-rus To the new-born King.

I o'er-heard a Mo-ther Was a-sing-ing 'Sweet Je-su,
And the Vir-gin-mo-ther Was a-sing-ing 'Sweet Je-su,
While the Vir-gin-mo-ther Was a-sing-ing 'Sweet Je-su,
Then the Vir-gin-mo-ther Fell a-sing-ing 'Sweet Je-su,   La-lul-lay-

-lu, La-lul-lay-lu, La-lul-lay-lu, Lul-lay la-lu.'

Words reprinted from *An Italian Carol Book* by permission of The Faith Press Ltd.

for The Bach Choir

36. BIRTHDAY CAROL

Words adapted from Luke ii

Words and music by
DAVID WILLCOCKS

†Children and/or Audience join in (optional)

Also available separately (X249)

Verses 2, 4, and 6

mf 2. Shep-herds a - bi - ding in the field,
f 4. 'Ti - dings of joy to you I bring,' *Al - le - lu -*
mf 6. A host of an - gels fill'd the sky,

To them God's glo - ry was re - veal'd.
- ia, 'To - day is born a heav'n - ly King.'
Thus sing - ing praise to God on high. *Al - le - lu - ia.*

f (Repeat p)

Glo - ri - a, Glo - ri - a
Glo - ri - a, Glo - ri - a in ex - cel - sis, Glo - ri - a, Glo - ri - a
Glo - ri - a, Glo - ri - a

Glo-ri-a, Glo - ri - a in ex - cel - sis, Glo - ri - a, Glo - ri - a

Verse 7 *(from previous page)*

ALL VOICES *ff*

7. Now join we all the an-gel throng, Al-le-lu-ia, And let our voi-ces swell the song: Al-le-lu-ia. Glo-ri-a, Glo-ri-a in ex-cel-sis, Glo-ri-a, Glo-ri-a

37. SALVE PUERULE★

(Welcome, thou holy child)

English words by
JOHN RUTTER

M. A. CHARPENTIER (1634—1704)
edited by JOHN RUTTER

OPTIONAL INTRODUCTION *(before Verse 1 only)*

VERSE 1: 1st time, soprano solo†; repeat full chorus
VERSE 2: 1st time, soprano solo (no repeat)
VERSE 3: 1st time, soprano solo; repeat full chorus

(Accompaniment doubles voice parts)

★from *In Nativitatem Domini Nostri Jesu Christi Canticum*

† The verses are sung in the cantata by each of the three kings in turn. They may be taken by three different
soloists, or alternatively sung by full sopranos.

es. Tu cae-lum de-fe-ris, Tu mun-do na-sce-ris, No-bis te ut
birth. *On thee our sins are laid, Son of a vir-gin maid, God-head in*

es. Tu cae-lum de-fe-ris, Tu mun-do na-sce-ris, No-bis te ut
birth. *On thee our sins are laid, Son of a vir-gin maid, God-head in*

after each verse:
to RITORNELLO on next page

mi-se-ris as-si-mi-les; No-bis te ut mi-se-ris as-si-mi-les.
flesh ar-rayed Come down to earth; God-head in flesh ar-rayed Come down to earth.

mi-se-ris as-si-mi-les; No-bis te ut mi-se-ris as-si-mi-les.
flesh ar-rayed Come down to earth; God-head in flesh ar-rayed Come down to earth.

2. O summa bonitas!
   Excelsa deitas
‖: Vilis humanitas
   Fit hodie. :‖
   Aeternus nascitur
   Immensus capitur
‖: Et rei tegitur
   Sub specie. :‖

3. Virgo puerpera
   Beata viscera
‖: Dei cum opera
   Dent filium. :‖
   Gaude, flos virginum,
   Gaude, spes hominum,
‖: Fons, lavans criminum
   Proluvium. :‖

2. *Sent down from God on high,*
   In humble crib to lie;
‖: *Ox and ass standing by*
   Jesus our Lord. :‖
   Day-star with brightest ray,
   Bear thou our sins away;
‖: *Saviour, to thee we pray,*
   By all adored. :‖

3. *Mary, thou blessed one,*
   Through thee God's will is done:
‖: *Bearing his only Son*
   This joyful morn. :‖
   Hail, queen of heaven bright!
   Shining with purest light;
‖: *Of thee, by God's great might,*
   Jesus is born. :‖

RITORNELLO *(after each verse)*

Editorial Method: Crossed slurs, material in square brackets, small notes, and the introduction (adapted from the *Ritornello*) are editorial.

38. STAR CAROL

Words and music by
JOHN RUTTER

1. Sing this night, for a boy is born in Beth-le-hem,
2. An-gels bright, come from hea-ven's high-est glo - ry,

1. Sing this night,____
2. An - gels bright,____

Christ our Lord in a low-ly man-ger lies;___ Bring your gifts, come and
Bear the news with its mes-sage of good cheer:___ "Sing, re - joice, for a

Christ our Lord____ Bring your gifts,____
Bear the news____ "Sing, re - joice,____

Children may join in the melody of the refrain, which is intended to be taught at the time of the performance.

Also available separately (X233) and in an arrangement for unison voices (U153)

© Oxford University Press 1972

wor-ship at his cra - dle, Hur-ry to Beth - le - hem and see the son of

King is come to save us, Hur-ry to Beth - le - hem and see the son of

Ma - ry!

Ma - ry!"

See his star shin-ing bright

A *REFRAIN* (children join in)
ALL VOICES

In the sky this Christ-mas Night! Fol-low me joy-ful-ly;

Hur - ry   to Beth - le - hem__ and see the son__ of   Ma - ry!

Ww.

2nd time
only

B ⌐1st time   ⌐2nd time

B ⌐1st time   tr   ⌐2nd time

mf   p dolce

C S.   p dolce e legato

3. See, he lies in his mo-ther's ten-der keep - ing; Je - sus Christ in her

A.   p dolce e legato

Ah___

T.   p dolce e legato

Ah___

B. Piano   p dolce e legato

Ah___   Ah___

lov-ing arms a-sleep. Shep-herds poor, come to wor-ship and a-dore_ him,

Ah__   Ah__

Ah__   Ah__

Ah__

Of-fer their hum-ble gifts__ be-fore the son__ of Ma - ry.

Ah__   Ah__

Ah__

p

D *REFRAIN*

p legato

See his star   shin - ing bright   In the sky this_

p legato

D

Christ-mas Night! Fol-low me___ joy-ful-ly;___ Hur-ry to Beth - le - hem___

___ and see the son___ of Ma - ry!

mf

E ALL VOICES

f

4. Let us all pay our hom-age at the man - ger,

Sing his praise on this joy-ful Christ-mas Night; Christ is come, bring-ing

pro-mise of sal-va - tion; Hur-ry to Beth - le - hem__ and see the son__ of

Ma - ry!

REFRAIN (ALL VOICES)

See his star shin-ing bright

Ped.   ✳   sim.

39. SHEPHERDS, IN THE FIELD ABIDING

Words by
G. R. WOODWARD

French traditional melody
arranged by DAVID WILLCOCKS

1. Shep-herds, in the field a-bid-ing, Tell us, when the
2. We be-held (it is no fa-ble) God in-car-nate,

Se-raph bright Greet-ed you with won-drous tid-ing,
King of bliss, Swathed and cra-dled in a sta-ble,

What ye saw and heard that night. Glo —
And the an-gel-strain was this: Glo —

— ri-a
— ri-a

Words reprinted by permission of A. R. Mowbray & Co. Ltd.

in__ ex - cel - sis De - o,___ Glo - - - - - - -

De - - o!
De - - o!
- - - - - ri - a   in __ ex - cel - sis   De - - o!

3. Quiristers on high were singing
   Jesus and his virgin-birth;
   Heav'nly bells the while a-ringing
   'Peace, goodwill to men on earth.'
   Gloria, etc.

4. Thanks, good herdmen; true your story;
   ★Have with you to Bethlehem:
   Angels hymn the King of Glory;
   Carol we with you and them.
   Gloria, etc.

★Have with you = I am ready to go with you.

40. SING WE TO THIS MERRY COMPANY

15th-century English
edited by
JOHN STEVENS

lievë = believe

Reproduced by permission of Stainer & Bell Ltd.

we:
- ty;   Re - gi - na___ cae - li, lae - - - ta - - - re.

we:
- ty;   Re - gi - na cae - li, lae - - ta - - - re.

VERSES 3, 4, and 5

3. Hail wife, hail mai - dë, bright___ of___ ble! Hail daugh-ter, hail sis - ter
4. Lo, this cour-teous King of___ de - gree Will be___ thy Son with
5. There-fore kneel we on___ our___ knee; Thy bliss - ful birth now

3. Hail wife, hail mai - dë, bright___ of __ ble! Hail daugh-ter, hail sis - ter
4. Lo, this cour-teous King of___ de - gree Will be___ thy Son with
5. There-fore kneel we on___ our __ knee; Thy bliss - ful birth now

full___ of pi - ty! Hail cou - sin to the__ Per-sons___ Three!___
so - lemp - ni - ty; Mild Ma - ry, this__ is thy___ fee;___
wor - - ship__ thee With this song of__ me - lo - dy:___

full of___ pi - ty! Hail cou - sin to the Per - sons Three!___
so - lemp - ni - ty; Mild Ma - ry, this is thy fee;___
wor - - - ship thee With this song of me - lo - dy:___

___   Re - gi - na___ cae - li, lae - - -ta - - - re.

___   Re - gi - na cae - li, lae - - -ta - - - re.

ble = countenance fee = reward

Transposed up a fourth from the edition in *Musica Britannica*, Vol. IV. Small accidentals, and underlay, are editorial.

The voice parts of both the burden and the verses may be doubled by suitable instruments.

If preferred, the burden may be sung thus: Top part — 1st sopranos doubled an octave lower by tenors.
Middle part — 2nd sopranos doubled an octave lower by 1st basses.
Bottom part — altos doubled an octave lower by 2nd basses.

41. STILLE NACHT
(Silent Night)

Words by JOSEPH MOHR,
tr. DAVID WILLCOCKS

FRANZ GRÜBER
arranged by DONALD CASHMORE

The English words are used by permission.
Also available separately (X 252)

© Oxford University Press 1975

Grüber: St

SOPRANO
ALTO

(hum throughout)

2. Stil - le Nacht, hei - li - ge Nacht! Hir - ten erst
2. *Si - lent night, ho - ly night, Shep - herds first*

TENOR
BASS 1
BASS 2

p (hum throughout)

kund ge - macht, Durch der En - gel Hal - le - lu - ja
saw the sight, Heard the an - gel-song al - le - lu - ia

Tönt es laut von fern und nah': Christ, der Ret - ter, ist
Loud pro - claim - ing near and far: Christ our Sa - viour is

D.C. for verse 3

da! Christ, der Ret - ter, ist da!
here, Christ our Sa - viour is here.

★Both sing words

2. GABRIEL'S MESSAGE

Basque Carol
arranged by DAVID WILLCOCKS

Ga - bri - el from hea - ven came, His
less - ed Mo - ther thou shalt be, All
Ma - ry meek - ly bowed her head, 'To
ma - nu - el, the Christ, was born In

Ah

wings as drift - ed snow, his eyes as flame; 'All
ge - ne - ra - tions laud and ho - nour thee, Thy
me be as it pleas - eth God,' she said, 'My
Beth - le - hem, all on a Christ - mas morn, And

Ah

Ah

hail,' said he, 'thou low - ly mai - den Ma - ry,
Son shall be Em - ma - nu - el, by seers fore - told,
soul shall laud and mag - ni - fy his ho - ly name.'
Chris - tian folk through-out the world will ev - er say:

} Most

Ah   Ah   Ah
Ah   Ah   Ah

Ah   Ah   Ah

high - ly fa - vour'd la - dy,   Glo - - - ri - a!

Ah   Ah   Glo - ri - a!

Ah   Glo - ri - a!

43. BOAR'S HEAD CAROL

English traditional carol
arranged by DAVID WILLCOCKS

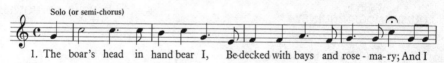

1. The boar's head in hand bear I, Be-decked with bays and rose - ma-ry; And I

pray you, my mas-ters, be mer-ry, *Quot es - tis in con - vi - vi - o:*

%REFRAIN (Chorus)   Fine

Ca - put a - pri de - fe - ro, Red-dens lau - des Do - mi - no.

2. The boar's head, as I un - der-stand, Is the rar-est dish in all this land, Which

REFRAIN D.S.

thus be-decked with a gay gar - land, Let us *ser - vi - re can - ti - co:*

3. Our ste-ward hath pro - vi - ded this, In ho - nour of the King of bliss, Which

REFRAIN D.S.

on this day to be ser - ved is, *In Re - gi - nen - si a - tri - o:*

For David and John

44. TRYSTE NOEL

Words by
LOUISE IMOGEN GUINEY

HERBERT HOWELLS

The ox he op·en·eth wide___ the door,___

___And from the snow___ he calls her in;___ And he hath seen___ her smile___ there-

But sore am I   with vain   tra - vel!

allarg.   **D** **poco meno mosso**

The ox is host in

allarg.   **D** *f* **poco meno mosso**

Ju - da's stall,   And   host _ of _ more than on - ly   one;

45. THERE IS NO ROSE

Words: 15th century

BENJAMIN BRITTEN

was Hea-ven and earth in li - tel space, Res mi - ran - da,___

___ Res mi - ran - da. By that rose we may well see

There be one God in per-sons three, Pa - res for - ma,___ pa - res

46. KING HEROD AND THE COCK

Words traditional

WILLIAM WALTON

thrustened = crowed

47. WHAT CHILD IS THIS?

Words by
W. C. DIX
and Editors★

English traditional melody
arranged by DAVID WILLCOCKS

† If preferred, the setting may be sung unaccompanied.
★Words from *English Praise* by permission of Oxford University Press

ⓒ Oxford University Press 1978

48. KINGS OF ORIENT

Words and tune by
J. H. HOPKINS
arranged by DAVID WILLCOCKS

1. We three kings of O - ri - ent are; Bear - ing gifts we tra - verse a - far Field and foun - tain, moor and moun - tain, Fol - low - ing yon - der star: O___ star of won - der, star of night, Star with roy - al beau - ty bright, West - ward lead - ing,

still pro - ceed - ing, Guide us to thy per - fect light.

(*Melchior*)
2. Born a king on Bethlehem plain,
   Gold I bring, to crown him again
   King for ever, ceasing never,
   Over us all to reign:
   O star of wonder, etc.

(*Caspar*)
3. Frankincense to offer have I;
   Incense owns a deity nigh:
   Prayer and praising, all men raising,
   Worship him, God most high:
   O star of wonder, etc.

(*Balthazar*)
4. Myrrh is mine; its bitter perfume
   Breathes a life of gathering gloom;
   Sorrowing, sighing, bleeding, dying,
   Sealed in the stone-cold tomb:
   O star of wonder, etc.

(*All*)
5. Glorious now, behold him arise,
   King, and God, and sacrifice!
   Heav'n sings alleluya,
   Alleluya the earth replies:
   O star of wonder, etc.

Verses 2, 3, and 4 may be sung by three different soloists whilst the choir accompanies, singing *Ah*.

for the Rt. Hon. Edward Heath

49. WHAT SWEETER MUSIC

Words by
ROBERT HERRICK

RICHARD RODNEY BENNETT

dar-ling of ___ the world is come, and fit it is we find a room ___ to

wel-come him. The nob - ler part ___ of all the house ___ here is the heart:

We see him come, and know him ours, who with his sun - shine
We see him come, and know him ours, who with his sun -

and his showers
- shine and his showers Turns all the pa - tient ground to flowers.

Which we will give him, and be - queath this hol - ly and this

50. THE CROWN OF ROSES

(Legend)

Words by PLECHTCHÉEV
tr. GEOFFREY DEARMER

P. I. TCHAIKOVSKY

1. When Je-sus Christ was yet a child He had a garden small and wild, Where-in he cher-ished ro-ses fair, And wove them in-to gar-lands there.

2. Now once, as sum-mer-time drew nigh, There came a troop of child-ren by, And see-ing ro-ses on the tree, With shouts they plucked them mer-ri-ly.

Translation from *The Oxford Book of Carols* by permission

3. 'Do you bind ro - ses   in __ your   hair?'__   They cried, in scorn, to
'Do   you bind ro - ses in   your   hair?' They cried,   in   scorn,   to

3. 'Do you bind ro - ses   in __ your   hair?'   They cried, in scorn, to

Je - sus   there.   The boy said hum -bly: 'Take, I   pray,   All but the

na   - ked thorns a - way.'   4. Then of the thorns they made   a   crown, And

with   rough fin - gers_ pressed it __ down, Till   on   his   fore -head fair   and

young Red drops of __ blood _____   like   ro - ses   sprung.__

like ro - ses sprung, like ro - ses sprung.__

App. 1. THIS JOYFUL EASTERTIDE

Words by
G. R. WOODWARD

Dutch carol
arranged by CHARLES WOOD

2. My flesh in hope shall rest,
    And for a season slumber:
Till trump from east to west
    Shall wake the dead in number.
    Had Christ, that once, etc.

3. Death's flood hath lost his chill,
    Since Jesus cross'd the river:
Lover of souls, from ill
    My passing soul deliver.
    Had Christ, that once, etc.

Words reprinted from *The Cowley Carol Book* by permission of A. R. Mowbray & Co. Ltd.

Processed and printed by Halstan & Co. Ltd., Amersham, Bucks., England

INDEX OF ORCHESTRATIONS

[ ] denotes optional instrument

Str   Strings
SO   Small Orchestra :- Strings, woodwind (2.2.2.1 [+1]), brass (2.2.0.0.), timpani
FO   Full Orchestra :- Strings, woodwind (2.2.2.2.), brass (4.3.3.1), timpani,
                          percussion
B5   Brass 1.2.1.1 [org]
B8   Brass 0.4.3.1 [org]

NO.   ORCHESTRATIONS AVAILABLE

1   FO/ [pno *or* celeste]
3, 9, 17, 30, 31   Str: SO: FO:B5:B8
5 (Chorale 1)   Str/[2.2.0.1]/0.3.0.0/timp/continuo
5 (Pastoral
Symphony and
Chorale 2)   Str/2.2.2 (*or* 2ca).[1]/0.0.0.0/continuo
6   Str/pno *or* org:SO/[perc]
7   Str:Str/2.2.0.1/2.0.0.0/hp
8   B8/perc
10   Str/2.2.2.1/2.0.0.0/[perc, hp]:2.0.1.1/0.0.0.0/[guitar]
12,37   Str/continuo
16   Str/2.2.2.1/2.0.0.0/[timp, glock, hp]
19   Str/2.2.2.1/2.0.0.0/perc/hp:2fl/claves/maracas/bass/pno *or* org
23   Str/2.2.2.1/2.0.0.0/perc/hp:B8/timp/perc/hp
24   Str/sd/tri
25   Str/1 (or picc).2.0.1/2.0.0.0/glock/hp
27   Str/1.[2].0.[1]/2.0.0.0/[perc]/hp/[org]
29   Str(2,2,2,1,1 *or* more)/fl/hp
32   Str:SO
36   SO/perc:B8/perc
38   Str/2(2nd doubling picc).2.2.2/2.0.0.0/[timp,perc,hp]
44, 47   Str

APPENDIX OF SUGGESTED CHRISTMAS POETRY READINGS

AUTHOR	FIRST LINE (*title*)
[1,2]ANONYMOUS	Adam lay y-bounden
[2]ANONYMOUS	Ay, ay, this is the day
[1,2]ANONYMOUS	Can I not sing but 'hoy'? (*The jolly Shepherd*)
[2]ANONYMOUS	Hay, ay, hay, ay (*Now is Yule come*)
[1,2]ANONYMOUS	I sing of a maiden
[2]ANONYMOUS	Lullay, my child
[2]ANONYMOUS	Make we mery, both more and lass (*Now is the Time of Christmas*)
[2]ANONYMOUS	Now have good day, now have good day (*I am Christmas*)
[2]ANONYMOUS	Of a rose, a lovely rose
[2]ANONYMOUS	This endris night (*Lullay, By-by, Lullay*)
[2]AUDELAY, JOHN	There is a flowr sprung of a tree (*The fairest Flower*)
[2]AUDELAY, JOHN	What tithinges bringest us, messangère (*What Tidings?*)
[4]BETJEMAN, SIR JOHN	The bells of waiting Advent ring (*Christmas*)
[4]ELIOT, T. S.	A cold coming we had of it (*Journey of the Magi*)
[4]FALKNER, JOHN MEADE	In the days of Caesar Augustus (*Christmas Day – The Family Sitting*)
[4]HARDY, THOMAS	Christmas Eve, and twelve of the clock (*The Oxen*)
[1,3]MILTON, JOHN	It was the winter wild (*Hymn on the Morning of Christ's Nativity*)
[2]RYMAN, JAMES	Fare wel Advent! Cristemas is cum
[2]RYMAN, JAMES	Mary hath born alone (*Mary and her son alone*)
[1]SMART, CHRISTOPHER	Where is this stupendous stranger? (*The Nativity of our Lord and Saviour*)
[1]SOUTHWELL, ROBERT	As I in hoary winter's night (*The Burning Babe*)
[1]SOUTHWELL, ROBERT	Behold, a silly tender Babe (*New Prince, New Pomp*)
[1]SOUTHWELL, ROBERT	Come to your heaven, you heavenly choir! (*New Heaven, New War*)

[1] in *The New Oxford Book of English Verse*
[2] in *The Oxford Book of Medieval English Verse*
[3] in *The Oxford Book of Seventeenth-Century Verse*
[4] in *The Oxford Book of Twentieth-Century English Verse*